SUKI
THE
SEAL

Kate Petty · Shona Grant

TED SMART

Suki was a Grey Seal pup, but her first baby fur was pure white. It glistened in the autumn sunshine as she lay on the beach waiting hungrily for the next feed.

First published 1990 by Walker Books Ltd
87 Vauxhall Walk, London SE11 5HJ

This edition produced for
The Book People Ltd, Hall Wood Avenue
Haydock, St Helens WA11 9UL

Printed in Hong Kong

ISBN 0-7445-1381-2

There were hundreds of baby seals in the rookery. Suki's mother could pick out Suki's cry from all the others, but she sniffed her just to make sure. With all that milk, Suki soon grew round as a barrel.

When Suki was three weeks old and beginning to lose her lovely white fur, a terrible thing happened. Her mother went away and left her. Suki couldn't even swim! How would she find her food?

Suki hauled herself clumsily down to the rock
pool. There was quite a gathering of motherless
pups. They shivered and shut their eyes tight as
they tested the icy water with their flippers.

Little by little, the pups learned to swim and look after themselves. For several days they played and splashed about together in the water. Suki even caught her first fish.

Two weeks later, Suki was ready for an adventure.
She set off to see the sea.
Suki swam twenty miles on that first day. She
popped her head out of the water to breathe and
looked around.

Suki's whiskers told her that fish were near.
Fishermen weren't always friendly, but
this one was.

Suki gripped the slippery fish with her claws
and ate it all up – except for the head.

Suki swam on and on. Sixty miles in two days!
She blew all the air out of her nostrils and her
ears, ready to dive. She could stay under for ten
minutes if she tried.

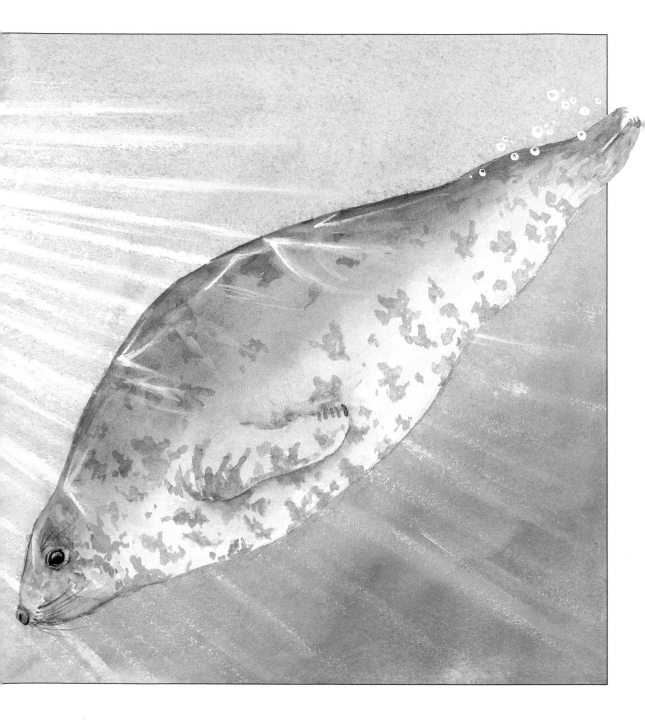

A net! Something warned Suki to keep away from all those tempting fish. These fishermen wouldn't like seals. Suki swam to the surface as fast as her flippers would take her.

Suki's first long journey was over. Wearily she hauled herself out on to the beach of the rookery where she was born. She basked on a rock in the wintry sun. The fish could wait.